Scales & Arpeggios for Piano

J Koh's Fingering Method

Grade 3

How To Use The Book

B major

R.H.	1	2♯	3♯	1	2♯	3♯	4♯	1	2♯	3♯	1	2♯	3♯	4♯	5
L.H.	4	3♯	2♯	1	4♯	3♯	2♯	1	3♯	2♯	1	4♯	3♯	2♯	1

Place the both hands on the key note B. Play the B major scale ascending, 2 octaves, according to the fingering indicated above. This scale requires five sharps, thus the fingering *2♯ 3♯ 4♯*. The highest note at the top of the scale is indicated with a box 5. Now play the scale descending, this time moving backwards. You will be surprised how quickly you learn your scales!

This method employs visual recognition of numerals with tactile co-ordination to assist the learning of scales and arpeggios. When playing hands together, **gaps** in the method refer to *turns led by the right hand*. Fingering of the left hand is placed in line with that of the right hand to ensure good co-ordination. Sharps are indicated on the right side of the fingering to show a raised note while flats are placed on the left for lowered notes. Effective rhythmic grouping is shown by notation on the staves.

Teachers and students are <u>not</u> obliged to follow the fingering patterns. Alternative fingering is occasionally provided in brackets. The size of hands and length of fingers vary and thus other alternatives are possible as long as a good legato touch, evenness of tone and smoothness of execution are achieved. Try to keep fingers curved and listen carefully to the sound produced. Metronome speeds are suggested for practice and examination purposes.

Josephine Koh

Published by
Wells Music Publishers
896 Dunearn Road
Sime Darby Centre #04-03
Singapore 589472

Cover design by Lee Kowling

Typesetting by Yvonne Choo and Mifiona Quah

Edited by David Saw

Scales & Arpeggios for Piano

GRADE 3

Major Scales of A, E, B, B♭ and E♭

Minor Scales of B, G and C

Contrary Motion of A major and A minor

Chromatic Scales on A♭ and C

Arpeggios of A, E, B, B♭ and E♭ majors, G, B and C minors

Major Scales

Hands separately and together: 2 octaves

Starter's speed ♪ = 108   Minimum exam speed ♩ = 80   Recommended speed ♩ = 88

A major

R.H.   1 2 3#   1 2 3# 4#   1 2 3#   1 2 3# 4# |5|

L.H.   5 4 3#   2 1 3# 2#   1 4 3#   2 1 3# 2# |1|

E major

R.H.   1 2# 3#   1 2 3# 4#   1 2# 3#   1 2 3# 4# |5|

L.H.   5 4# 3#   2 1 3# 2#   1 4# 3#   2 1 3# 2# |1|

B major

R.H.	1	2#	3#	1	2#	3#	4#	1	2#	3#	1	2#	3#	4#	5
L.H.	4	3#	2#	1	4#	3#	2#	1	3#	2#	1	4#	3#	2#	1

B♭ major

R.H.	♭2	1	2	♭3	1	2	3	♭4	1	2	♭3	1	2	3	♭4
L.H.	♭3	2	1	♭4	3	2	1	♭3	2	1	♭4	3	2	1	♭2

E♭ major

R.H.	♭2	1	2	♭3	♭4	1	2	♭3	1	2	♭3	♭4	1	2	♭3
L.H.	♭3	2	1	♭4	♭3	2	1	♭3	2	1	♭4	♭3	2	1	♭2

Minor Scales

Hands separately and together: 2 octaves
Candidates can choose either melodic or harmonic

Starter's speed ♪ = 108   Minimum exam speed ♩ = 80   Recommended speed ♩ = 88

B melodic minor

R.H.   1 2# 3   1 2# 3# 4#   1 2# 3   1 2# 3# 4# [5]

L.H.   4 3# 2   1 4# 3# 2#   1 3# 2   1 4# 3# 2# [1]

        4 3 2# 1   3 2# 1   4 3 2# 1   3 2# [1]

        2 3 4# 1   2 3# 1   2 3 4# 1   2 3# [4]

OR

B harmonic minor

R.H.   1 2# 3   1 2# 3 4#   1 2# 3   1 2# 3 4# [5]

L.H.   4 3# 2   1 4# 3 2#   1 3# 2   1 4# 3 2# [1]

G melodic minor

R.H.   1 2 ♭3   1 2 3 4#   1 2 ♭3   1 2 3 4# 5̲

L.H.   5 4 ♭3   2 1 3 2#   1 4 ♭3   2 1 3 2# 1̲

               4 ♭3 2 1   ♭3 2 1   4 ♭3 2 1   ♭3 2 1̲

               2 ♭3 1 2   ♭3 4 1   2 ♭3 1 2   ♭3 4 5̲

OR

G harmonic minor

R.H.   1 2 ♭3   1 2 ♭3 4#   1 2 ♭3   1 2 ♭3 4# 5̲

L.H.   5 4 ♭3   2 1 ♭3 2#   1 4 ♭3   2 1 ♭3 2# 1̲

C melodic minor

R.H. 1 2 ♭3 1 2 3 4 1 2 ♭3 1 2 3 4 [5]

L.H. 5 4 ♭3 2 1 3 2 1 4 ♭3 2 1 3 2 [1]

♭4 ♭3 2 1 ♭3 2 1 ♭4 ♭3 2 1 ♭3 2 [1]

♭2 ♭3 1 2 ♭3 4 1 ♭2 ♭3 1 2 ♭3 4 [5]

OR

C harmonic minor

R.H. 1 2 ♭3 1 2 ♭3 4 1 2 ♭3 1 2 ♭3 4 [5]

L.H. 5 4 ♭3 2 1 ♭3 2 1 4 ♭3 2 1 ♭3 2 [1]

Contrary Motion

Hands together, beginning and ending on key note: 2 octaves

Starter's speed ♪ = 108   Minimum exam speed ♩ = 80   Recommended speed ♩ = 88

A major

R.H.   1 2 3#   1 2 3# 4#   1 2 3#   1 2 3# 4# $\boxed{5}$

L.H.   1 2# 3#   1 2 3# 4   1 2# 3#   1 2 3# 4 $\boxed{5}$

A minor

R.H.   1 2 3   1 2 3 4#   1 2 3   1 2 3 4# $\boxed{5}$

L.H.   1 2# 3   1 2 3 4   1 2# 3   1 2 3 4 $\boxed{5}$

Chromatic Scales

Hands separately: 2 octaves

Starter's speed ♪ = 120   Minimum exam speed ♩ = 80   Recommended speed ♩ = 96

✓ **Beginning on A♭ (Only 1 octave is shown)**

R.H.   ♭3 1 ♭3 1 2 ♭3 1 ♭3 1 2 ♭3 1 [♭3]

L.H.   ♭3 1 ♭3 2 1 ♭3 1 ♭3 2 1 ♭3 1 [♭3]

✓ **Beginning on C**

R.H.   1 ♭3 1 ♭3 1 2 3♯ 1 ♭3 1 ♭3 1 [2]

L.H.   1 ♭3 1 ♭3 2 1 3♯ 1 ♭3 1 ♭3 2 [1]

Arpeggios
Hands together in root position: 2 octaves

Starter's speed ♪ = 96   Minimum exam speed ♩ = 69   Recommended speed ♩ = 72

A major   A C# E

R.H.		1	2#	3	1	2#	3	5

L.H.		5	(3#)	2	1	(3#)	2	1
			(4#)			(4#)		

G minor

R.H.		1	♭2	3	1	♭2	3	5

L.H.		5	♭3	2	1	♭3	2	1
			(♭4)			(♭4)		

Hands separately in root position: 2 octaves

E major E G# B

R.H.   1   2#   3   1   2#   3   5

L.H.   5   3#   2   1   3#   2   1
                 (4#)   (4#)

B major B D# F#

R.H.   1   2#   3#   1   2#   3#   5

L.H.   5   3#   2#   1   3#   2#   1
                 (4#)   (4#)

11

B♭ major B♭ D F

R.H.   ♭2   1   2   ♭4   1   2   ♭4

L.H.   ♭3   2   1   ♭3   2   1   ♭2
        (♭4)   (♭4)

E♭ major E♭ G B♭

R.H.   ♭2   1   ♭2   ♭4   1   ♭2   ♭4

L.H.   ♭2   1   ♭4   ♭2   1   ♭4   ♭2
        (♭3)

12

B minor

R.H.   *1*   *2*   *3#*   *1*   *2*   *3#* $\boxed{5}$

L.H.   *5*   *4*   *2#*   *1*   *4*   *2#* $\boxed{1}$
           (3)   *(3)*

C minor

R.H.   *1*   *♭2*   *3*   *1*   *♭2*   *3* $\boxed{5}$

L.H.   *5*   *♭3*   *2*   *1*   *♭3*   *2* $\boxed{1}$
           (♭4)   *(♭4)*

END

13

Best-Selling Titles

Teachers' Choice, Selected Piano Repertory
Examination Pieces for 2009-2010 Series
Edited and Annotated by Josephine Koh

A refreshing new publication which comprises popular and alternative works from the ABRSM Piano Examination syllabus. These pieces are specially selected to provide students with a comprehensive and varied repertoire. Meticulously fingered and edited, *Teachers' Choice* offers teachers and students alike added performance and teaching directions. Scores in *Teachers' Choice* are beautifully set and annotated for excellent reading.

Available from Grades 1 to 8.

Practice in Music Theory
Revised Edition
by Josephine Koh

The revised edition of the *Practice in Music Theory* series is a set of highly recommended instructional workbooks for students who wish obtain a sound foundation in music theory. The *J Koh's* teaching approach is academic and logical, yet musically conceived. Progressive topics are set out to guide students through their understanding of the fundamental musical concepts and ideas. Based on the requirements of the ABRSM theory syllabus, this Grade 2 book contains:

- clear teaching points and graphical illustrations
- explanatory notes that are consistently applied throughout the series
- exercises of progressive difficulty that provide students with sufficient practice to master the topics and concepts learnt
- updated information and study notes that are most effective for reference and revision.

Available from Grades 1 to 8.

Rhythmatics
by Josephine Koh

Group notes, write beats, identify time signatures and complete bars with missing notes or rests — all these tasks with Rhythmatics, the most sought after musical learning aid for young children. Attractive colour cards, each with a particular colour and shape corresponds to a specific time value. With the cards to be arranged on the base whiteboard mathematically, the child visualises the concept instantaneously and is able to perceive the number of beats in a bar. Most suitable for children between ages of 4 to 9, Rhythmatics is recommended for the study of music theory up to Grade 2.